DEPARTMENT OF THE NAVY
HEADQUARTERS UNITED STATES MARINE CORPS
2 NAVY ANNEX
WASHINGTON, DC 20380-1775

I0430096

ENLISTED-TO-OFFICER COMMISSIONING PROGRAMS

DEPARTMENT OF THE NAVY
HEADQUARTERS UNITED STATES MARINE CORPS
2 NAVY ANNEX
WASHINGTON, DC 20380-1775

MCO 1040.43A
MCRC OE
2 May 00

MARINE CORPS ORDER 1040.43A

From: Commandant of the Marine Corps
To: Distribution List

Subj: ENLISTED-TO-OFFICER COMMISSIONING PROGRAMS

Ref: (a) MCO 1300.8R
       (b) MCO 6100.3J
       (c) ManMed, Chap. 15 (NOTAL)
       (d) MCO P1020.34F
       (e) MCO P1530.8C (NOTAL)
       (f) SECNAVINST 5510.30A (NOTAL)
       (g) MC0 7220.24M
       (h) MCO P1070.12J
       (i) MCO 1542.1F
       (j) SECNAVINST 5212.5C

Encl: (1) Enlisted Commissioning Program (ECP)
       (2) Meritorious Commissioning Program (MCP)
       (3) Common Problems with Medical Forms
       (4) Information for Commanding Officers

1. Purpose. To set forth the requirements and regulations of the Enlisted Commissioning Program and the Meritorious Commissioning Program.

    a. The ECP allows qualified enlisted Marines in the Regular Marine Corps and in the Marine Corps Active Reserve (AR) Program to apply for assignment to Officer Candidates School (OCS) and subsequent appointment to unrestricted commissioned officer grade in the U.S. Marine Corps Reserve.

    b. The MCP allows commanding officers to nominate highly qualified enlisted Marines in the Regular Marine Corps and the Active Reserve Program, who do not possess a baccalaureate degree, who have demonstrated exceptional leadership potential, for assignment to OCS and subsequent commissioning in the Marine Corps Reserve.

2. Cancellation. MCO 1040.43.

DISTRIBUTION STATEMENT A: Approved for public release; distribution is unlimited.

3. <u>Summary of Revision</u>. This order updates the application format to include submission of tattoo photographs and Service Record Book (SRB) page 11 entry regarding fraternization. In addition, waivers will be permitted for the maximum age and minimum test score requirements. The minimum academic requirement has been raised to 75 semester hours. There are other minor administrative changes throughout the order.

4. <u>Information</u>

   a. These programs are intended to provide an opportunity to gain commissioned status as unrestricted reserve officers. These programs also provide an aviation option to qualified applicants. These programs are not intended to serve as a commissioning program for Marines who are better suited to serve as warrant officers.

   b. <u>Deadline</u>

      (1) All applications will be submitted for consideration to selection boards convened by direction of the Commandant of the Marine Corps to select the best qualified for commissioning.

      (2) Selection boards convene a maximum of three times per year. An annual selection board schedule will be released by MARADMIN announcing the application deadlines, board convening dates, and training periods. Female applicants will not be considered for the winter OCS class due to non-availability of training facilities.

      (3) Applications will be mailed to:

         Commanding General
         Marine Corps Recruiting Command (OE)
         3280 Russell Road
         Quantico, VA 22134-5103

   c. Those Marines selected to attend OCS receive a commission after successful completion of OCS. Subsequent to commissioning, the new officer will be ordered to attend The Basic School.

5. <u>Eligibility</u>. Marines applying for assignment to an officer candidate class under the provisions of this order must meet the following requirements in addition to those listed in enclosures (1) or (2):

a. General Qualifications

(1) Be a citizen of the United States.

(2) Be of unquestionable moral integrity and have no record of conviction by a general, special, or summary court-martial, nor have any record of conviction by a court for any offense, other than minor traffic violations. The term "conviction" includes a finding of guilt or other pretrial adjudication (including a conditional dismissal of charges, pretrial diversion, plea of nolo contendre, etc., by a Federal, state or foreign court, whether or not a sentence was imposed, the conviction was later expunged, or the record of the court's disposition was sealed. Consult MCO P1100.73B for detailed guidance regarding disclosure of criminal offense dispositions.

(3) Not have previously failed to complete any military officer program. Applicants dropped at their own request or for physical reasons during training must reapply and will be considered on a case-by-case basis, if recommended for return by the Commanding Officer, OCS. Additionally, aviation applicants must not have previously failed any military flight training program.

(4) Have executed a waiver of rights, if entitled to a restrictive assignment as defined in reference (a).

(5) Must have attained a passing score on the most recent physical fitness test (PFT) per reference (b).

(6) Must possess one of the following aptitude test scores:

(a) Scholastic Aptitude Test (SAT) - minimum combined Math and Verbal score of 1000; or

(b) American College Test (ACT) - minimum combined Math and English score of 45; or

(c) Armed Forces Classification Test (AFCT) - a minimum converted score of 115 on the Electrical Composite (EL). Previous forms of the Armed Services Vocational Aptitude Battery (ASVAB) may still be used, provided they are not older than 14 November 1976. Only EL scores in the Marine Corps Total Force System (MCTFS) listed on the Basic Training Record (BTR) or test score screen will be accepted.

3

(7) In addition to one of the above, aviation candidates must attain a minimum converted score of 4/6/4 on the U.S. Navy and Marine Corps Aviation Selection Test Battery (ASTB).

(8) Ground candidates must be at least 21 years of age and less than 30 years of age on date of appointment to commissioned grade. Aviation candidates must be at least 21 years of age and less than 27 1/2 years of age on date of appointment to commissioned grade. Waivers up to the legal limits of age 35 will be considered on exceptionally well qualified ground applicants. Waivers for aviation applicants will be considered up to age 29 as of the date of commissioning.

b. Academics

(1) Must possess a high school diploma (or a GED certificate issued by a state department of education).

(2) MCP applicants must have satisfactorily earned an associate level degree or completed 75 semester hours or more of unduplicated college work at a regionally accredited college or university. Nontraditional credits given for tests (i.e., CLEP, DANTES, etc.), service schools, or MCI courses cannot be included in the initial minimum requirement, unless they are included into an associate level degree. Waivers will be considered on a case-by-case basis down to 60 semester hours for highly qualified nominees. Subsequent to commissioning it will be incumbent on the Marine to continue progressing toward a 4-year baccalaureate degree to be competitive for augmentation and promotion.

(3) ECP applicants must have satisfactorily earned a baccalaureate level degree from a regionally accredited college or university prior to applying for the program.

(4) Enlisted Marines possessing a 4-year degree are not eligible for MCP.

c. Physical

(1) Ground Officer Applicants. Must be found physically qualified for appointment to commissioned grade in the U.S. Marine Corps Reserve per the standards set forth in reference (c). Waivers may be considered under the policy described in paragraph 15-3 of reference (c).

(2) <u>Naval Aviator Applicants</u>. Must be found physically qualified and aeronautically adapted for duty involving actual control of aircraft and qualified for appointment to commissioned grade under paragraph 5c(1) above. See paragraph 20 of this order for additional guidance on physical qualifications.

(3) <u>Naval Flight Officer Applicants</u>. Must be found physically qualified and aeronautically adapted for duty as a Naval Flight Officer and qualified for appointment to commissioned grade under paragraph 4c(1) above. See paragraph 20 of this order for additional guidance on physical qualifications.

(4) Commanding officers must closely review the medical forms to ensure correctness and completeness. Enclosure (3) contains a list of the most common items overlooked or misunderstood.

d. <u>Service Requirement</u>

(1) Marines on active duty must have completed a minimum of 1 year active Marine Corps service and have at least 12 months remaining on current enlistment or extension on the date of application. The minimum active duty requirement may be waived for exceptionally well qualified recruit training graduates based on the recommendation of the commanding general of the recruit depot.

(2) Marine Reservists serving within the AR Program are eligible to apply provided they are willing to accept release from the AR Program.

6. <u>Tattoos, Brandings, piercings</u>

a. The Marine Corps takes a conservative approach to personal appearance. Uniform regulations stress that personal appearance is to be conservative and commensurate with the high standards traditionally associated with the Marine Corps. No eccentricities in dress or appearance are permitted because they detract from uniformity and team identity.

b. Per reference (d), the Marine Corps uniform regulations prohibit tattoos or brands on the neck and the head. Additionally, any tattoo that is gang, racist, sexist, or drug related is prohibited. In other areas of the body, tattoos or brands that are prejudicial to good order, discipline, and morale, or are of a nature to bring discredit upon the Marine Corps, are also prohibited.

c. tattoos, body piercing, and non-dental tooth crowns are identified as body art, and commanders are tasked with upholding current regulations regarding eccentric appearance.

(1) Four criteria will be used to evaluate tattoos and brands to see if they comply with Marine Corps standards. These criteria are content, location, size, and effect of associating the Marine Corps and the Marine Corps uniform with the tattoo or brand.

(2) In order for the selection board to evaluate the tattoos and brands, the Marine must provide appropriate color photos which clearly identifies the tattoo, or brand, along with a description detailing location, size, and number of tattoos. In cases where the tattoo is in a private area, a written description will suffice.

d. Commanders must screen all tattoos to ensure they meet the above criteria. The commander must state in the first endorsement, "I have viewed the applicant's tattoos or brands (photos and/or description) attached as enclosure (xx) and they are within the Marine Corps standards per the Marine Corps Uniform Regulations."

7. Precommissioning Training Agreement. Approved candidates are required to participate in officer candidate training for a minimum of seven weeks before any voluntary request for disenrollment will be considered. Reference (e) authorizes the Commanding Officer, OCS, to effect involuntary disenrollment for cause during any phase of officer candidate training.

8. Security Investigation. Per reference (f), candidates must have a current National Agency Check with Local Agency Check and Credit Check (NACLC), or higher level security investigation prior to commissioning. In view of the short training period, the following action will preclude administrative delays in the acceptance of a commission.

a. If there has been a security investigation conducted during the current contract, reenlistment, or extension, no further action is necessary. Include evidence of the investigation as an enclosure to the application if it is not indicated on the Basic Training Record (BTR).

b. If a security investigation is not current, initiate a personnel security investigation per reference (f).

c. If an investigation request has already been initiated, the commanding officer should indicate the date the request was initiated in the endorsement of the application.

9. Fraternization

a. The Marine Corps has had great success with "grow-our-own" enlisted-to-officer programs. These successful programs give the Marine Corps a broad-based, highly experienced officer corps. One unintended consequence of this success, however, relates to fraternization.

b. Navy Regulations, Chapter 11, General Regulations, Section 5 (Rights and Restrictions) par. 1165 (Fraternization Prohibited) states, "Personal relationships between officer and enlisted members that are unduly familiar and that do not respect differences in grade or rank are prohibited. Such relationships are prejudicial to good order and discipline and violate longstanding traditions of the Naval Service." Fraternization may be charged as an offense under the Uniform Code of Military Justice. The only exceptions are familial relationships, defined as marriages that occur prior to the date of commission or appointment and relationships between parents and children or between siblings.

c. To prevent fraternization or the appearance of fraternization, it is imperative that our enlisted Marines are briefed on the Marine Corps guidelines relating to fraternization. Therefore, commanders are required to ensure that each Marine applying for an enlisted to officer program reads and understands the Marine Corps policy on fraternization. Each Marine must sign the following SRB, page 11 entry and submit a certified true copy as part of the application:

"I have read and understand the Marine Corps policy on fraternization. I understand that, as a commissioned or warrant officer, I will be required to conduct myself as an officer with respect to all enlisted personnel, of any service, at all times. Specifically, I understand that I may have to make significant changes in my current personal relationships with other service members if I become an officer. I also understand that fraternization is an offense under the UCMJ, and that the prohibition of fraternization does not make an exception for preexisting relationships other than marriages that took place prior to my date of commission or appointment to warrant officer or other family relationships, such as that between parents and children or between siblings."

10. <u>Selective Reenlistment Bonus Payment (SRBP)</u>. An application for an enlisted-to-officer commissioning program is not a bar to bonus entitlement for either the initial payment or the anniversary installment payment. Generally, upon appointment as an officer, further payments cease, but recoupment is not required. Reference (g) provides further definitive guidance and should be consulted directly.

11. <u>Submission of Applications</u>. Submit applications (ORIGINAL ONLY) using the sample formats and forms contained in enclosure (1) or (2). Include a current photograph following the guidance in reference (h) regarding promotion photos.

12. <u>Action of Commanding Officers</u>

    a. Commanding officers are responsible for exercising close and continuous supervision over these programs while ensuring all eligible enlisted Marines are afforded the opportunity to apply for ECP. MCP presupposes a nomination of a highly qualified Marine and nomination packages should not be forwarded unless the Marine is highly recommended.

    b. Should a commanding officer desire to modify the original endorsement, immediately notify the Commanding General, Marine Corps Recruiting Command (OE).

    c. Subsequent to submission of an application, should a weight gain or loss, injury or illness occur that may affect the individual's physical qualifications for appointment to commissioned grade, obtain a medical consultation and forward the results immediately to the Commanding General, Marine Corps Recruiting Command (OE).

    d. If, at any time after submission of an application, an applicant (pending or approved) is the subject of an investigation or disciplinary action, notify the Commanding General, Marine Corps Recruiting Command (OE) immediately.

    e. The maintenance of a strong motivation for commissioned service and a high state of physical fitness for approved candidates awaiting assignment to OCS is essential. Enclosure (4) provides information and material for use by commanding officers in preparing candidates for transition to an officer training environment. Imaginative use of enclosure (4) will enhance the professional attitude and enthusiasm of candidates reporting to OCS.

13. <u>Interview Board</u>. Upon receipt of an application, the commanding officer in the chain of command having special court-martial convening authority will convene an interview board. The board will consist of a minimum of three officers. If available, at least one member of the board will be an officer of the same sex as the applicant being interviewed. If available, a minority officer will be a member of the board interviewing minority applicants. The board will interview the applicant and make an appropriate recommendation to the convening authority concerning the applicant's potential for commissioned service, characteristics, communicative skills, and motivation for flight training. Appendix E of enclosures (1) and (2) contain a sample Interview Board Report.

14. <u>Transfer of Pending Applicants</u>

    a. Marines undergoing temporary duty under instruction (TEMINS), whose applications have been completed and forwarded, will not be placed in a hold status by the field command pending final disposition of the application by the Commanding General, Marine Corps Recruiting Command.

    b. If an applicant receives permanent change of station orders after submission of an application and prior to notification of final disposition by the Marine Corps Recruiting Command, the commanding officer will request resolution by message (NAVGRAM during MINIMIZE) to the Commandant of the Marine Corps (MMEA) and info the Commanding General, MCRC (OE).

15. <u>Withdrawal of Application</u>

    a. Applicants must submit written notification of withdrawal of application to the Commanding General, Marine Corps Recruiting Command (OE), should they no longer desire consideration.

    b. Candidates in receipt of orders to officer candidate training who desire to withdraw may do so, but only prior to executing their orders. Commanding officers will advise the Commanding General, Marine Corps Recruiting Command (OE) of such withdrawal by message followed by correspondence enclosing the applicant's signed and witnessed withdrawal statement.

16. <u>Selection/Nonselection</u>. Applicants will be notified of the action taken on their application by MARADMIN. Ineligible applications will be returned without further action.

17. Approved Officer Candidates

   a. Marines selected for these programs will be assigned to a
specified 10-week officer candidate class conducted at the Marine Corps
Combat Development Command (MCCDC), Quantico, Virginia, on the dates
prescribed by the Commandant of the Marine Corps.

   b. Marines selected for these programs must ensure all remediation of
dental defects, to include correction of caries, partial plates, caps,
root canals, and extractions are completed prior to reporting to training.

18. Appointment to Commissioned Grade

   a. Candidates who successfully complete OCS and who are recommended
by the Commanding General, MCCDC, Quantico, Virginia, will be appointed to
the grade of second lieutenant in the U.S. Marine Corps Reserve. All
newly appointed officers will be further assigned to The Basic School for
commissioned officer training.

   b. Per the specific ECP/MCP Service Agreement, the officer is
required to serve at least eight years in the Marine Corps Reserve from
the date of appointment to commissioned grade. Any portion of this eight-
year period not served on active duty will be served on inactive duty as a
member of the Marine Corps Reserve. A resignation of a reserve commission
submitted prior to completion of this eight-year period will normally be
rejected and, after this period, may be accepted or rejected by the
resident as the needs of the service may then require.

19. Unsuccessful Candidates. Candidates who do not complete
precommissioning training will be reassigned per reference (e). Active
duty personnel will be required to complete their current service
obligation. Former AR enlisted Marines will remain in an Individual Ready
Reserve status. A former AR enlisted Marine will not be returned to
active duty with the AR Program unless subsequently selected by an AR
selection board.

20. <u>Naval Aviator (NA) and Naval Flight Officer (NFO) Training</u>.
For purposes of identification, ECP (NA) candidates will be designated
ECP (A), ECP (NFO) candidates will be designated ECP (N) and MCP (NA)
candidates will be designated MCP (A). NFO training is not an option
for MCP.

    a. <u>Qualifications</u>

       (1) Personnel assigned to flight training must meet the
criteria defined in reference (i).

       (2) To ensure prospective commissioned officers meet the
required mental and physical qualifications for flight training,
the following actions will be completed on all aviation applications:

          (a) Completion of a flight physical examination per
reference (c), chapter 15, section V.

          (b) Satisfactory completion of the ASTB. Aviation
selection tests may be administered by Marine officer selection
officers or designated naval flight surgeons. Applicants who
fail to attain the minimum score of 4/6/4 on the AQR/PFAR/PBI
may not retest for at least 30 days for the first retest, and 180
days for subsequent retests. No waivers of the test score will be
granted.

          (c) Completion of proper service agreement.

    b. <u>Assignments</u>

       (1) Aviation candidates, upon commissioning, will be
assigned to The Basic School (TBS) prior to flight training.

       (2) Ground officers attending TBS may request assignment
to an aviation training program; those qualified will be evaluated
along with their contemporaries, on the basis of demonstrated performance
in officer candidate training and The Basic School.

21. Records Disposition

a. Pertinent information from the application and supporting documents will be incorporated into a database management system (DBMS) upon receipt by the Marine Corps Recruiting Command (OE). The record will be resident in the DBMS until it is archived. Additionally, a paper report from the DBMS will become a permanent (SSIC 1040) file governed by reference (j).

b. Applications and supporting documents of selectees will be retained until incorporated into the Official Military Personnel File and the Officer Qualification Record and then destroyed.

c. Applications and supporting documents of nonselectees will be destroyed 90 days after final decision of the selection board.

d. Commanding officers who submit the first endorsement will retain a record copy of the application and supporting documents for one year from the date of the endorsement.

22. Reserve Applicability. This order is applicable to the Marine Corps Reserve.

GARRY L. PARKS
By direction

DISTRIBUTION: PCN 10200281400

Copy to: 7000110 (55)
          7000124 (50)
          7000120 (3)
          7000093, 8145005 (2)
          7000099, 144/8145001 (1)

ENLISTED COMMISSIONING PROGRAM (ECP)

1. <u>Application Checklist</u>. Applications must contain the following enclosures, if applicable:

    a. <u>Application Cover Letter</u>. Follow the sample format shown in Appendix A.

    b. <u>Application Form</u>. Appendix B should be locally reproduced, completed by the applicant, and witnessed by the commanding officer.

    c. <u>Service Agreement</u>. Appendix C contains the specific service agreements for the commissioning options. Submit the appropriate service agreement (in duplicate with original signatures) for ground or aviation. Aviation applicants should submit both ground and aviation agreements along with a statement stating whether the applicant will accept a ground contract in the event there are no aviation vacancies or the candidate is found not qualified for aviation.

    d. <u>Data Sheet</u>. Appendix D is a data sheet which will reduce the amount of time required to prepare each application for the board. The data sheet will be used for computer entry purposes by MCRC personnel only. The data sheet will be the second enclosure to the package.

    e. <u>Interview Board Report</u>. Follow the guidance in paragraph 13 of this order and sample format for the Report of Interview Board contained in Appendix E.

    f. <u>Academic Certification Form (ACF)</u>. The applicant should locally reproduce the ACF contained in Appendix F, then forward it to the registrar of the most recent school attended for completion. Be sure to provide a self-addressed, stamped envelope to the registrar to facilitate return of this form along with official transcripts.

    g. <u>Transcripts of all College Grades/Credits</u>. Transcripts must bear the official seal of the school. Photostats or other legible copies are acceptable provided they are marked "certified true copy."

    h. <u>Evidence of Baccalaureate Degree</u>. Should the transcript contain this information, it is not necessary to submit this enclosure.

i. Report of Medical Examination (SF88) and Report of Medical History (SF93)

(1) Ground Applicants. Ground applicants must send the completed SF88 and SF93, original plus one copy, directly to the Commanding General, Marine Corps Recruiting Command (OE) in advance. Retain one certified copy of each to include as an enclosure to the application. The SF88 and SF93 should be clearly marked "ECP (G) APPLICANT" in Block 5.

(2) Aviation Applicants. Aviation applicants will have a flight physical examination conducted by a flight surgeon. Forward the completed SF88 and SF93 for processing (original plus one) directly to the Commanding General, Marine Corps Recruiting Command (OE) in advance. Retain one certified true copy of each as an enclosure to the application. The SF88 and SF93 should be clearly marked "ECP (NA) OR ECP (NFO) APPLICANT" in Block 5.

j. Handwritten Statement. Each applicant must submit an essay (100 words or less) on why he or she would make a good officer. The handwritten statement must be signed by the applicant. Do not type or print.

k. Submit a recent photograph per reference (g).

l. Certified copies of the following current service record book (SRB) pages:

(1) Chronological Record (NAVMC 118 (3))

(2) Education Record (NAVMC 118 (8a))

(3) Awards Record (NAVMC 118(9))

(4) Administrative Remarks (NAVMC 118 (11))

(5) Offenses and Punishments (NAVMC 118 (12))

ENCLOSURE (1)

m. The following computer generated screens from MCTFS:

   (1) Basic individual Record (BIR)

   (2) Basic Training Record (BTR)

   (3) Record of Service (ROS)

   (4) Education Record (EDU)

n. If applicable, waiver of restrictive assignment rights.

o. <u>Evidence of Official SAT or ACT Scores, if applicable</u>. If the college transcripts or the ACF contain SAT or ACT scores, it is not necessary to submit the college report of test scores. For reporting scores directly to MCRC (OE), use code 5825.

p. If the applicant is a foreign-born, naturalized citizen, ensure correct citizenship code is listed on the BIR or submit a Certificate of Proof of Citizenship (NAVMC 538).

q. <u>Endorsement</u>. Commanding officers must review applications for completeness, ensure applicants requesting waivers receive comprehensive justification on all endorsements, and make definitive recommendations regarding the Marine's leadership qualities and potential for commissioned service. The immediate commanding officer must follow the sample format contained in Appendix G.

SAMPLE ECP APPLICATION COVER LETTER

1040
DATE

From: Grade, Full Name, SSN, PMOS/USMC
To: Commanding General, Marine Corps Recruiting Command (OE)
Via: (1) Commanding Officer
      (2) Endorsing chain of command

Subj: APPLICATION FOR THE ENLISTED COMMISSIONING PROGRAM

Ref: (a) MCO 1040.43A

Encl: (1) ECP Application Form
      (2) Data Sheet
      (3) Academic Certification Form
      (4) Official Transcripts w/Evidence of Degree
      (5) SF 88, SF 93, and Support Documents
      (6) Report of Interview Board Report
      (7) Handwritten Statement
      (8) Service Agreement
      (9) Photograph
      (10) SRB, pages 3, 8a, 9, 11, and 12
      (11) MCTFS Screens BIR, BTR, ROS, and EDU
      (12) List any additional enclosures that apply

1. I request to be considered for the Enlisted Commissioning
Program and assignment to Officer Candidates School. Per the
reference, enclosures (1) through (12) are submitted.

2. In this paragraph, any applicant that requires a waiver
must request the waiver and provide justification. If no waivers
are required, omit this paragraph.

3. In this paragraph, an applicant for an aviation guarantee
must state whether or not there is a willingness to accept a
ground commission in the event there are no aviation vacancies or
the applicant is not found to be best qualified for aviation.
If the applicant is willing to accept a ground commission, submit
both the aviation and ground service agreements.

Signature of Applicant

ECP APPLICATION FORM

DATE:

1. SSN	2. NAME (LAST, FIRST, MIDDLE (MAIDEN) JR., ETC)	3. PRES GRADE	4. PMOS

5. DATE AND PLACE OF BIRTH (CITY, ST)	MARITAL STATUS AND DEPENDENTS	6. SEX	7. R/E	8. CITIZEN	9. PEBD

10. SCHOOL INFORMATION	11. CURRENT DUTY STATION (COMPLETE ADDRESS)

A. COLLEGE / UNIVERSITY WHERE DEGREE WAS AWARDED	B. CODE	C. EDUC/MAJ
	D. GPA	E. GRAD DTE

POC: (NAME & BILLET)

12. EAS DATE	13. HOME OF RECORD (CITY, COUNTY, ST)

PHONE: (DSN & COMMERCIAL)

14. PGM CODE	15. OCS CLASS	16. PFT SCORE PU	CR	RUN TIME	17. WAIVERS REQUIRED / /	18. FY	19. PROJ COMM DATE

20. TEST SCORES

A. ASVAB/AFCT COMPOSITE SCORES							B. SAT
GT	GM	EL	CL	MM	CO	FA	MATH / VERBAL / COMB
							/ /

C. ACT ENGL/MATH/COMB	D. AVIATION AQR /FAR /BI	21. RELATIVES WHO SERVED/SERVING IN THE ARMED SERVICE
/ /	/ /	

	YES	NO			YES	NO
A. HAVE YOU EVER APPLIED FOR OR BEEN A MEMBER OF ANY ROTC OR OTHER TYPE OF OFFICER CANDIDATE PROGRAM?			E. HAVE YOU EVER BEEN PSYCHOLOGICALLY OR PHYSICALLY DEPENDENT UPON ANY DRUG OR ALCOHOL?			
B. HAVE YOU EVER FAILED IN ANY MILITARY FLIGHT TRAINING PROGRAM?			F. ARE YOU A CONSCIENTIOUS OBJECTOR?			
C. ARE YOU A "SOLE SURVIVING" SON?			G. HAVE YOU EVER USED NONPRESCRIBED OR ILLEGAL DRUGS?			
D. HAVE YOU EVER BEEN ARRESTED, CONVICTED OR SENTENCED BY A COURT?			H. HAVE YOU EVER BEEN A TRAFFICKER OF ILLEGAL DRUGS?			

"YES" ANSWERS TO ANY OF THE ABOVE QUESTIONS, ATTACH A STATEMENT EXPLAINING THE CIRCUMSTANCES.

I CERTIFY THAT THE INFORMATION CONTAINED IN THIS APPLICATION IS TRUE, COMPLETE, AND CORRECT TO THE BEST OF MY KNOWLEDGE AND BELIEF. I UNDERSTAND THAT KNOWING AND WILLFUL FALSE STATEMENTS ON THIS FORM CAN BE PUNISHED BY A FINE OR IMPRISONMENT OR BOTH. (SEE U.S. CODE TITLE 18, SECTION 1001.)

APPLICANT'S SIGNATURE _____

(SIGNATURE OF COMMANDING OFFICER)

TYPED NAME AND GRADE OF CO

INSTRUCTIONS FOR COMPLETION OF APPLICATION FOR THE ENLISTED
COMMISSIONING PROGRAM (ECP)

Most of the items on this form are self-explanatory.
The following lists items which may need more explanation.
The majority of these items can be found on SNM's BIR/BTR:

-- Block 4 - PMOS: Primary military occupational specialty.

-- Block 7 - R/E: Race/Ethnic Codes.

-- Block 9 - PEBD: Pay Entry Base Date.

-- Block 10b - CODE: College Code - Leave Blank.

-- Block 10c - EDUC/MAJ: Education Level and Major Subject.
Use one-digit code indicating the type of certificate issued
followed by the two-digit code indicating the major subject of
study.

-- Block 10d - GPA: Grade Point Average.

-- Block 10e - GRAD DTE: Graduation Date.

-- Block 12 - EAS DATE: Expiration of Active Service.
Six-digit date the SNM's active service is to expire.

-- Block 13 - HOME OF RECORD: Legal home of record as
listed in MCTFS.

-- Block 14 - PGM CODE: Program Code. Male applicants
use 4I followed by either (A) for Naval Aviation, (N) for
Naval Flight Officer or (G) for ground option. Female
applicants use 1EW.

-- Block 16 - PFT SCORE: Provide total points attained and
number of pull ups, number of crunches, and run time.

-- Block 17 - WAIVERS REQUIRED: Enlistment waivers must be
renewed. Use the following codes: AY - AGE; CY - Test scores;
DD - Moral; DG - Drugs; DH - Alcohol; and HY - Physical.

-- Block 18 - FY: Fiscal Year.

-- Block 19 - PROJ COMM: Projected commission date. (As published
in the annual MARADMIN announcing the selection board schedule.

APPENDIX B to
ENCLOSURE (1)

SERVICE AGREEMENT
ENLISTED COMMISSIONING PROGRAM (GROUND OFFICER)
==

1. In connection with my application for enrollment in the
ENLISTED COMMISSIONING PROGRAM (GROUND OFFICER) of the United
States Marine Corps, I hereby acknowledge:

    a. That final approval of my nomination for enrollment in
the Enlisted Commissioning Program, as an officer candidate,
will be determined by the Commandant of the Marine Corps.

    b. That upon reporting to an officer candidate class, I
will be required to participate in training for a minimum period
of seven weeks, unless sooner disenrolled for cause, before any
voluntary request for disenrollment will be considered.

    c. That, as a regular Marine, if I fail to satisfactorily
complete the requirements for appointment to commissioned grade
or request disenrollment from an officer candidate class prior to
acceptance of a commission, I will be required to complete my
enlistment contract, including any extension thereof and any
obligated period of extended active duty.

    d. That, as a reserve Marine, if I am released from the AR
Program to attend OCS, I realize if I fail to satisfactorily
complete the requirements for appointment to commissioned grade
or request disenrollment from an officer candidate class prior to
acceptance of a commission, I will not be returned to active duty
with the AR Program. I understand my status will be that of a
member of the Individual Ready Reserve.

    e. That, upon satisfactory completion of all requirements,
I will accept appointment to commissioned grade in the United
States Marine Corps Reserve, if a commission is tendered to me.

    f. That:

        (1) A commission in the Marine Corps Reserve is for an
indefinite term and is held during the pleasure of the President;

        (2) Upon acceptance of a commission, I will be required
to serve at least eight years in the Marine Corps Reserve from date
of appointment to commissioned grade;

        (3) Any portion of this eight-year period not served on
active duty will be served on inactive duty as a member of the
Marine Corps Reserve; and

APPENDIX C to
ENCLOSURE (1)

(4) A resignation of my reserve commission submitted prior to completion of this eight-year period will normally be rejected and, after this period, may be accepted or rejected by the President as the needs of the service may then require.

g. Upon acceptance of appointment to commissioned grade, I will be further assigned to The Basic School for commissioned officer training.

h. Assignment to an officer candidate class should not be construed as approval for future assignment to flight or aviation training.

i. Sections 671a and 671b of Title 10, United States Code, currently provide as follows:

"671a. Members: Service extension during war. Unless terminated at an earlier date by the Secretary concerned, the period of active service of any member of an armed force is extended for the duration of any war in which the United States may be engaged and for six months thereafter.

"671b. Members: Service extension when Congress is not in session.

"(a) Notwithstanding any other provision of law when the President determines that the national interest so requires, he may, if Congress is not in session, having adjourned *sine die*, authorize the Secretary of Defense to extend for not more than six months enlistments, appointments, periods of active duty, periods of obligated service or other military status, in any component of the Armed Forces of the United States, that expire before the thirtieth day after Congress next convenes or reconvenes.

"(b) An extension under this section continues until the sixtieth day after Congress next convenes or reconvenes or until expiration of the period of extension specified by the Secretary of Defense, whichever occurs earlier, unless sooner terminated by law or Executive Order."

j. Federal statutes and pertinent regulations applicable to personnel in the Marine Corps may change without notice and that such changes may affect my status as an officer candidate or commissioned officer and obligations to serve as such.

APPENDIX C to
ENCLOSURE (1)

2. I consent to serve on extended active duty, as a commissioned officer, for a minimum of three and one-half years from the date of appointment to commissioned grade, and understand that a request for release from active duty prior to completion of this period will be rejected.

3. I have read and completely understand the meaning and content of the above. Furthermore, I have read and understand the current Marine Corps Order pertaining to this program. No promises, either written or oral, have been made to me in connection with my application for enrollment in the Enlisted Commissioning Program (Ground Officer) except as specified above. I acknowledge receipt of a copy of this document.

Signature of Witnessing Officer   Applicant's Signature

_____   _____
Typed Name, Grade, SSN of Witness   Typed Name, SSN of Applicant

_____
        Date

SERVICE AGREEMENT
ENLISTED COMMISSIONING PROGRAM (NAVAL AVIATOR)
==
1. In connection with my application for enrollment in the
ENLISTED COMMISSIONING PROGRAM (NAVAL AVIATOR) of the United
States Marine Corps, I hereby acknowledge:

    a. That, final approval of my application for enrollment in
the Enlisted Commissioning Program (Naval Aviator), as an officer
candidate, will be determined by the Commandant of the Marine Corps.

    b. That, upon reporting to an officer candidate class, I will
be required to participate in training for a minimum period of seven
weeks, unless sooner disenrolled for cause, before any voluntary request
for disenrollment will be considered.

    c. That, as a regular Marine, if I fail to satisfactorily complete
the requirements for appointment to commissioned grade or request
disenrollment from an officer candidate class prior to acceptance of
a commission, I will be required to complete my enlistment contract,
including any extension thereof and any obligated period of extended
active duty.

    d. That, as a reserve Marine, if I am released from the AR
Program to attend OCS, I realize if I fail to satisfactorily
complete the requirements for appointment to commissioned grade
or request disenrollment from an officer candidate class prior to
acceptance of a commission, I will not be returned to active duty
with the AR Program. I understand my status will be that of a member
of the Individual Ready Reserve.

    e. That, upon satisfactory completion of all requirements, I
will accept appointment to commissioned grade in the United
States Marine Corps Reserve, if a commission is tendered to me.

    f. That:

        (1) A commission in the Marine Corps Reserve is for an
indefinite term and is held during the pleasure of the President;

        (2) Upon acceptance of a commission, I will be required
to serve at least eight years in the Marine Corps Reserve from date
of appointment to commissioned grade;

(3) Any portion of this eight-year period not served on active duty will be served on inactive duty as a member of the Marine Corps Reserve; and

(4) A resignation of my reserve commission submitted prior to completion of this eight-year period will normally be rejected and, after this period, may be accepted or rejected by the President as the needs of the service may then require.

g. Upon successful completion of the officer candidate course and acceptance of appointment to commissioned grade, I will be further assigned MOS 7599 (Naval Aviator Student) and will be assigned to The Basic School for commissioned officer training prior to my assignment to flight training.

h. Upon successful completion of the Basic School, I will be assigned to Student Naval Aviator Training, provided I am physically qualified for such assignment at that time.

i. Sections 671a and 671b of Title 10, United States Code, currently provide as follows:

"671a. Members: service extension during war. Unless terminated at an earlier date by the Secretary concerned, the period of active service of any member of an armed force is extended for the duration of any war in which the United States may be engaged and for six months thereafter.

"671b. Members: service extension when Congress is not in session.

"(a) Notwithstanding any other provision of law when the President determines that the national interest so requires, he may, if Congress is not in session, having adjourned *sine die*, authorize the Secretary of Defense to extend for not more than six months enlistments, appointments, periods of active duty, periods of obligated service or other military status, in any component of the Armed Forces of the United States, that expire before the thirtieth day after Congress next convenes or reconvenes.

"(b) An extension under this section continues until the sixtieth day after Congress next convenes or reconvenes or until expiration of the period of extension specified by the Secretary of Defense, whichever occurs earlier, unless sooner terminated by law or Executive Order."

j. Federal statues and pertinent regulations applicable to personnel in the Marine Corps may change without notice and that such changes may affect my status as an officer candidate or commissioned officer and obligations to serve as such.

2. I consent to serve on extended active duty, as a commissioned officer, for the following minimum periods and understand that a request for release from active duty prior to completion of these minimum periods will normally be rejected:

a. Ninety-six months from date of designation as a Naval Aviator if trained as a fixed wing pilot.

b. Seventy-two months from date of designation as a Naval Aviator if trained as a rotary wing pilot.

3. I have read and completely understand the meaning and content of the above. Furthermore, I have read and understand the current Marine Corps Order pertaining to this program. No promises, either written or oral, have been made to me in connection with my application for enrollment in the Enlisted Commissioning Program (Naval Aviator) except as specified above. I acknowledge receipt of a copy of this document.

Signature of Witnessing Officer   Signature of Applicant

_____   _____

Typed Name, Grade, SSN of witness   Typed Name, SSN of Applicant

_____

Date

APPENDIX C to
ENCLOSURE (1)

6

SERVICE AGREEMENT
ENLISTED COMMISSIONING PROGRAM (NAVAL FLIGHT OFFICER)
===

1. In connection with my application for enrollment in the
ENLISTED COMMISSIONING PROGRAM (NAVAL FLIGHT OFFICER) of the
United States Marine Corps, I hereby acknowledge:

    a. That, final approval of my application for enrollment in
the Enlisted Commissioning Program (Naval Flight Officer), as an
officer candidate, will be determined by the Commandant of the
Marine Corps.

    b. That, upon reporting to an officer candidate class, I will
be required to participate in training for a minimum period of seven
weeks, unless sooner disenrolled for cause, before any voluntary request
for disenrollment will be considered.

    c. That, as a regular Marine, if I fail to satisfactorily complete
the requirements for appointment to commissioned grade or request
disenrollment from an officer candidate class prior to acceptance of
a commission, I will be required to complete my enlistment contract,
including any extension thereof and any obligated period of extended
active duty.

    d. That, as a reserve Marine, if I am released from the AR
Program to attend OCS, I realize if I fail to satisfactorily
complete the requirements for appointment to commissioned grade
or request disenrollment from an officer candidate class prior to
acceptance of a commission, I will not be returned to active duty
with the AR Program. I understand my status will be that of a
member of the Individual Ready Reserve.

    e. That, upon satisfactory completion of all requirements, I
will accept appointment to commissioned grade in the United States
Marine Corps Reserve, if a commission is tendered to me.

    f. That:

        (1) A commission in the Marine Corps Reserve is for an
indefinite term and is held during the pleasure of the President;

        (2) Upon acceptance of a commission, I will be required
to serve at least eight years in the Marine Corps Reserve from date
of appointment to commissioned grade;

(3) Any portion of this eight-year period not served on active duty will be served on inactive duty as a member of the Marine Corps Reserve; and

(4) A resignation of my reserve commission submitted prior to completion of this eight-year period will normally be rejected and, after this period, may be accepted or rejected by the President as the needs of the service may then require.

g. Upon successful completion of the officer candidate course and acceptance of appointment to commissioned grade, I will be further assigned MOS 7580 (Student Naval Flight Officer) and will be assigned to The Basic School for commissioned officer training prior to my assignment to flight training.

h. Upon successful completion of the Basic School, I will be assigned to Student Naval Flight Officer training, provided I am physically qualified for such assignment at that time.

i. Sections 671a and 671b of Title 10, United States Code, currently provide as follows:

"671a. Members: service extension during war. Unless terminated at an earlier date by the Secretary concerned, the period of active service of any member of an armed force is extended for the duration of any war in which the United States may be engaged and for six months thereafter.

"671b. Members: service extension when Congress is not in session.

"(a) Notwithstanding any other provision of law when the President determines that the national interest so requires, he may, if Congress is not in session, having adjourned *sine die*, authorize the Secretary of Defense to extend for not more than six months enlistments, appointments, periods of active duty, periods of obligated service or other military status, in any component of the Armed Forces of the United States, that expire before the thirtieth day after Congress next convenes or reconvenes.

"(b) An extension under this section continues until the sixtieth day after Congress next convenes or reconvenes or until expiration of the period of extension specified by the Secretary of Defense, whichever occurs earlier, unless sooner terminated by law or Executive Order."

APPENDIX C to
ENCLOSURE (1)

    j. Federal statues and pertinent regulations applicable to
personnel in the Marine Corps may change without notice and that
such changes may affect my status as an officer candidate or
commissioned officer and obligations to serve as such.

2. I consent to serve on extended active duty, as a commissioned
officer, for seventy-two months from date of designation as a Naval
Flight Officer and understand that a request for release from active
duty prior to completion of this minimum period will normally be
rejected:

3. I further agree that in the event I am separated from flight
training as a result of flight failure, practical work failure, or
physical disqualification, I will serve on active duty in a commissioned
status for a period of four years from the date initially assigned to
active duty as a commissioned officer.

4. I further agree that in the event I am separated from flight training
as a result of my own request or by reason of academic failure, I will
serve on active duty in a commissioned status for a period of four years
from the date initially assigned to active duty as a commissioned officer,
plus an extension of active service equal to the time spent in flight
training.

5. I have read and completely understand the meaning and content
of the above. Furthermore, I have read and understand the current Marine
Corps Order pertaining to this program. No promises, either written or
oral, have been made to me in connection with my application for
enrollment in the Enlisted Commissioning Program (Naval Flight Officer)
except as specified above. I acknowledge receipt of a copy of this
document.

Signature of Witnessing Officer   Signature of Applicant

_____   _____
Typed Name, Grade, SSN of witness   Typed Name, SSN of Applicant

_____
    Date

DATA SHEET

INSTRUCTIONS: This enclosure is to be locally reproduced.
Applicant must complete items A through M column 2. Data sheet
will be used solely for computer entry purposes. Type in all
capital letters, no punctuation.

COLUMN 1   COLUMN 2

A. FULL NAME: (LAST, FIRST, MI)

B. SSN: (no spaces)

C. PRESENT PAY GRADE: (E?)

D. PRESENT MOS:

E. RACE/ETHNIC CODE: (see BIR)

F. AGE: (years, months)
    (As of date of commission)

G. EL/SAT/ACT TEST SCORES

H. PFT SCORE

    NO. OF PULL UPS

    NO. OF CRUNCHES

    RUN TIME

I. COLLEGE GRADUATED

J. MAJOR SUBJECT

K. CUMULATIVE GRADE POINT AVERAGE

L. GRADUATION DATE (YYMMDD)

M. TIME IN SERVICE: (years, months)
    (As of date of application)

SAMPLE REPORT OF LOCAL INTERVIEW BOARD

(To be completed by the local interview board on each applicant for the Enlisted Commissioning Program.)

1. Command convening board: _____

                                        _____ (List full address)

                                        _____

2. Name of applicant: _____
                                        (Last) (First) (M.I.)

                                        _____
                                        (Grade/Rank) (SSN) (MOS)

3. Date of present grade: _____

4. The applicant named above appeared before the interview board on (date) and the following comments constitute the opinion of a majority of the members.

    a. MANNER, APPEARANCE, BEARING: (Comment appropriately on the applicant's military presence, appearance, and bearing. Is it above, below, or at the standard generally expected of a Marine officer?)

    b. VOICE, LANGUAGE EXPRESSION, ALERTNESS, ABILITY TO COMMUNICATE: (Comment appropriately on the applicant's ability to convey clear, concise, and intelligent expressions. Does the applicant readily understand the meaning of questions?)

    c. PROFESSIONAL KNOWLEDGE: (Comment on the applicant's military proficiency, general knowledge of the Marine Corps, and social and civic awareness.)

    d. SELF-CONFIDENCE, PERSONALITY, MOTIVATION: (Comment on the applicant's degree of self-confidence, exhibited personality, and motivation for commission.)

    e. OTHER QUALIFICATIONS: (Does the applicant possess qualifications, not previously reported, that would be of particular value as an officer?)

5. <u>RECOMMENDATION</u>: (Name of Applicant) is recommended with (enthusiasm) (confidence) (reservation) or (not recommended) for appointment to commissioned grade as a second lieutenant in the U.S. Marine Corps Reserve. (Make a summary evaluation of the applicant's qualifications and potential for commissioned service.)

6. <u>MEMBERS OF THE INTERVIEW BOARD</u>:

Member: (Full name, grade, component)

Member: (Full name, grade, component)

Member: (Full name, grade, component)

                                                                   _____
                                                       Signature of Senior Member

APPENDIX E
ENCLOSURE (1)

ACADEMIC CERTIFICATION FOR ENLISTED COMMISSIONING PROGRAM

NAME OF STUDENT | SOCIAL SECURITY NUMBER
_____|_____

COLLEGE OR UNIVERSITY

_____

     This is to certify that the above named subject:

     Was _____ / Was not _____ a regularly enrolled full-time
student at this institution.

     The above-named student completed requirements for the
following degree:

     _____ Associate _____ Baccalaureate _____ Masters

     Date of completion of degree requirements: _____

     The below information is required to determine this
student's eligibility for admission to, or retention in, the
U.S. Marine Corps Enlisted Commissioning Program:

          MAJOR SUBJECT _____
          TOTAL NUMBER OF HOURS ATTEMPTED _____
          TOTAL NUMBER OF HOURS COMPLETED _____
          TOTAL NUMBER OF GRADE POINTS ACHIEVED _____
          CUMULATIVE GRADE POINT AVERAGE (GPA) _____

          AT THIS INSTITUTION A GPA OF _____
          IS EQUIVALENT TO A "C."

          SAT SCORE: MATH _____ VERBAL _____
          ACT SCORE: MATH _____ ENGLISH _____

     It is requested that a certified copy of the student's
transcript be returned with this form.

     REMARKS:
                    SIGNATURE _____

     PLEASE   TITLE _____
AFFIX
       SEAL   DATE _____

MCO 1040.43A
2 May 00

COMPLETE MAILING ADDRESS
OF COLLEGE/UNIVERSITY
INCLUDING ZIP

Dear Registrar,

The student whose name appears on the enclosed form has applied
for enrollment in the U.S. Marine Corps Enlisted Commissioning
Program. Since a minimum grade point average is required for
admission to, or retention in our programs, I am requesting your
cooperation in furnishing essential information on this
individual's academic status.

I realize many demands are made upon your time, but please be
assured the Marine Corps relies on this information in the
decision process.

Enclosed is an addressed, postage-free envelope for your
convenience in returning this form.

                          Sincerely,

==
I am aware of the provisions of the Family Education Rights
Act. I hereby authorize the release of the requested information
and an official transcript directly to the Marine Corps agency
indicated on this form.

_____   _____   _____
(Signature of Witness)   (Signature of Applicant)   (Date)

APPENDIX F
ENCLOSURE (1)

FIRST ENDORSEMENT on (Grade, Full Name)`s ECP application
                   of (date)

From: Commanding Officer, (Unit)
To: Commanding General, Marine Corps Recruiting Command (OE)
Via: (1) Commanding Officer, (Battalion, Squadron, etc.)
       (2) Commanding General, (Division, Wing, Group, etc.)

Subj: APPLICATION FOR THE ENLISTED COMMISSIONING PROGRAM

1. The information contained in the basic application and the
enclosures thereto has been verified with records on file in
this command and are correct. The applicant meets the basic
eligibility requirements (except for (type of waiver)) for the
Enlisted Commissioning Program.

2. The height and weight of the applicant is (inches) and
(pounds). Applicant (does/does not) meet the medical and/or
dental qualifications. The applicant last took the PFT on (date)
and obtained the following score:

        Pull ups/Flex Arm Hang   20 (100)
        Crunches   100 (100)
        Run   18:00 (100)
        Total   300 (1st Class)

3. Provide a recommendation statement using one of the following
categories:

    a. Recommended with enthusiasm.

    b. Recommended with confidence.

    c. Recommended with reservation.

    d. Not recommended.

The recommendation must be fully justified by the commanding officer.
Provide an analysis of the applicant's potential for commissioned service
and any waiver requested.

4. The applicant has served in this command _____ months and has
_____ months remaining on current enlistment or extension thereof.

5. "I have viewed the applicant's tattoos or brands (photos and/or description) attached as enclosure (xx) and they are within the Marine Corps standards per the Marine Corps Uniform Regulations." (Omit this paragraph if it does not apply.)

6. The applicant's NAC was initiated on (date). (Only use this paragraph if NAC has not been completed.)

7. Unit telephone number and point of contact: (Indicate your administrative office's commercial and DSN numbers.)

(Signature of CO)

APPENDIX G to
ENCLOSURE (1)

MERITORIOUS COMMISSIONING PROGRAM (MCP)

1. <u>Nomination Checklist</u>. Nomination packages must contain the following enclosures, if applicable:

    a. <u>Nomination Cover Letter</u>. Follow the sample format shown in Appendix A.

    b. <u>Nomination Form</u>. Appendix B should be locally reproduced, completed by the nominee, and witnessed by the commanding officer.

    c. <u>Service Agreement</u>. Appendix C contains the specific service agreements for the commissioning options. Submit the appropriate service agreement (in duplicate with original signatures) for ground or aviation. Aviation applicants should submit both ground and aviation agreements along with a statement stating whether the applicant will accept a ground contract in the event there are no aviation vacancies.

    d. <u>Data Sheet</u>. Appendix D is a data sheet which will reduce the amount of time required to prepare each application for the board. The data sheet will be used for computer entry purposes by MCRC personnel only. The data sheet will be the first enclosure to the package.

    e. <u>Interview Board Report</u>. Follow the guidance in paragraph 13 of this order and sample format for the Report of Interview Board contained in Appendix E.

    f. <u>Academic Certification Form (ACF)</u>. The applicant should locally reproduce the ACF contained in Appendix F, then forward it to the registrar of the most recent school attended for completion. Be sure to provide a self-addressed, stamped envelope to the registrar to facilitate return of this form along with official transcripts.

    g. <u>Transcripts of all College Grades/Credits</u>. Transcripts must bear the official seal of the school. Photostats or other legible copies are acceptable provided they are marked "certified true copy."

    h. <u>Evidence of Associate Degree</u>. Should the transcript contain this information, it is not necessary to submit this enclosure.

i. Report of Medical Examination (SF88) and Report of Medical History (SF93).

(1) Ground Applicants. Ground applicants must send the completed SF88 and SF93, original plus one copy, directly to the Commanding General, Marine Corps Recruiting Command (OE), 3280 Russell Road, Quantico, VA 22134-5103 in advance. Retain one certified copy of each to include as an enclosure to the application. The SF88 and SF93 should be clearly marked "MCP (G) APPLICANT" in Block 5.

(2) Aviation Applicants. Aviation applicants will have a flight physical examination conducted by a flight surgeon. Forward the completed SF88 and SF93, original plus one, directly to the Commanding General, Marine Corps Recruiting Command (OE), 3280 Russell Road, Quantico, VA 22134-5103 in advance. Retain one certified true copy of each as an enclosure to the application. The SF88 and SF93 should be clearly marked "MCP (NA) APPLICANT" in Block 5.

j. Handwritten Statement. Each applicant must submit an essay (100 words or less) on why he or she would make a good officer. The handwritten statement must be signed by the applicant. Do not type or print.

k. Submit a recent photograph per reference (g).

l. Certified copies of the following current service record book (SRB) pages

(1) Chronological Record (NAVMC 118 (3))

(2) Education Record (NAVMC 118 (8a))

(3) Awards Record (NAVMC 118(9))

(4) Administrative Remarks (NAVMC 118 (11))

(5) Offenses and Punishments (NAVMC 118 (12))

m. The following computer generated screens from the Manpower Management System:

    (1) Basic Individual Record (BIR)

    (2) Basic Training Record (BTR)

    (3) Record of Service (ROS)

    (4) Education Record (EDU)

n. If applicable, waiver of restrictive assignment rights.

o. Evidence of Official SAT or ACT Scores, if applicable. If the college transcripts or the ACF contain SAT or ACT scores, it is not necessary to submit the college report of test scores. For reporting test scores directly to MCRC (OE), use code 5825.

p. If the applicant is a foreign-born naturalized citizen, ensure correct citizenship code is listed on the BIR or submit a Certificate of Proof of Citizenship (NAVMC 538).

q. Commanders must review applications for completeness, ensure nominees requiring waivers receive comprehensive justification on all endorsements, and make definitive recommendations regarding the Marines leadership qualities and potential for commissioned service.

ENCLOSURE (2)

3

SAMPLE NOMINATION COVER LETTER

1040
Code
DATE

From: Commanding Officer, (Unit)
To: Commanding General, Marine Corps Recruiting Command (OE)
Via: Endorsing chain of command

Subj: NOMINATION FOR THE MERITORIOUS COMMISSIONING PROGRAM OF
        CORPORAL I. M. MARINE 123 45 6789/0100 USMC

Ref: (a) MCO 1040.43A

Encl: (1) Data sheet
        (2) Nomination Form
        (3) List all other supporting enclosures as required

1. The information contained herein and enclosures (1) through (x) have
been verified with records on file at this command and are correct. The
nominee meets the basic eligibility requirements for the Meritorious
Commissioning Program.

2. The height and weight of the nominee is (inches) and (pounds).
The Marine (does/does not) meet the medical and/or dental qualifications.
 The Marine last took the PFT on (date) and obtained the following score:

            Pull ups/Flex Arm Hang   20 (100)
            Crunches   100 (100)
            Run   18:00 (100)
            Total   300 (1st Class)

3. Provide a recommendation statement. The recommendation must
be fully justified by the commanding officer. Provide an analysis
of the nominee's potential for commissioned service.

4. If a nominee requires a waiver, provide justification in this paragraph. If no waivers are required, omit this paragraph.

5. The Marine has served in this command ____ months and has ____ months remaining on current enlistment or extension thereof.

6. "I have viewed the applicant's tattoos or brands (photos and/r description) attached as enclosure (xx) and they are within the Marine Corps standards per the Marine Corps Uniform Regulations." (Omit this paragraph if it does not apply.)

7. The Marine's NAC was initiated on (date). (Only use this paragraph if NAC has not been completed.)

8. Per the reference, enclosure (X) contains the Interview Board Report.

9. Point of contact for administrative purposes is (NAME) at DSN XXX-XXXX and commercial (XXX) XXX-XXXX.

(Signature of CO)

APPENDIX A to
ENCLOSURE (2)

MCP APPLICATION FORMAT

DATE:

| 1 | 2. NAME (LAST, FIRST, MIDDLE (MAIDEN) JR., ETC) | 3. PRES GRADE | 4. PMOS |

| AND PLACE OF BIRTH (CITY, ST) | MARITAL STATUS AND DEPENDENTS | 6. SEX | 7. R/E | 8. CITIZEN | 9. PEBD |

| CCL INFORMATION | | 11. CURRENT DUTY STATION (COMPLETE ADDRESS) |

| COLLEGE / UNIVERSITY LAST ATTENDED | B. CODE | C. EDUC/MAJ |
| | D. GPA | E. GRAD DTE |

POC: (NAME & BILLET)

| DATE | 13. HOME OF RECORD (CITY, COUNTY, ST) | PHONE: (DSN & COMMERCIAL) |

| M DE | 15. OCS CLASS | 16. PFT SCORE PU | CR | RUN TIME | 17. WAIVERS REQUIRED | 18. FY | 19. PROJ COMM DATE |

20. TEST SCORES

| A. ASVAB/AFCT COMPOSITE SCORES | | | | | | B. SAT |
| GM | EL | CL | MM | CO | EA | MATH / VERBAL / COMB |

| ACT MATH/COMB | C. AVIATION AQR /FAR /BI | 21. RELATIVES WHO SERVED/SERVING IN THE ARMED SERVICE |

		YES	NO			YES	NO
YOU EVER APPLIED FOR OR BEEN MEMBER OF ANY ROTC OR OTHER TYPE OFFICER CANDIDATE PROGRAM?				E. HAVE YOU EVER BEEN PSYCHOLOGICALLY OR PHYSICALLY DEPENDENT UPON ANY DRUG OR ALCOHOL?			
YOU EVER FAILED IN ANY TARY FLIGHT TRAINING PROGRAM?				F. ARE YOU A CONSCIENTIOUS OBJECTOR?			
YOU A "SOLE SURVIVING" SON?				G. HAVE YOU EVER USED NONPRESCRIBED OR ILLEGAL DRUGS?			
YOU EVER BEEN ARRESTED, VICTED OR SENTENCED BY A COURT?				H. HAVE YOU EVER BEEN A TRAFFICKER OF ILLEGAL DRUGS?			

YES" ANSWERS TO ANY OF THE ABOVE QUESTIONS, ATTACH A STATEMENT EXPLAINING THE CIRCUMSTANCES.

RTIFY THAT THE INFORMATION CONTAINED IN THIS ICATION IS TRUE, COMPLETE, AND CORRECT TO THE OF MY KNOWLEDGE AND BELIEF. I UNDERSTAND THAT ING AND WILLFUL FALSE STATEMENTS ON THIS FORM BE PUNISHED BY A FINE OR IMPRISONMENT OR BOTH. U.S. CODE TITLE 18, SECTION 1001.)

(SIGNATURE OF COMMANDING OFFICER)

ICANT'S ATURE _____

TYPED NAME AND GRADE OF CO

APPENDIX B to
ENCLOSURE (2)

1

I INSTRUCTIONS FOR COMPLETION OF NOMINATION FOR THE
MERITORIOUS COMMISSIONING PROGRAM (MCP)

Most of the items on this form are self-explanatory.
The following lists items which may need more explanation.
The majority of these items can be found on SNM's BIR/BTR:

-- Block 4 - PMOS: Primary military occupational specialty.

-- Block 7 - R/E: Race/Ethnic codes.

-- Block 9 - PEBD: Pay Entry Base Date.

-- Block 10b - CODE: College Code - Leave Blank.

-- Block 10c - EDUC/MAJ: Education Level and Major Subject.
Use one-digit code indicating the type of certificate
issued followed by the two-digit code indicating the
major subject of study.

-- Block 10d - GPA: Grade Point Average.

-- Block 10e - GRAD DTE: Projected Graduation Date.

-- Block 12 - EAS DATE: Expiration of Active Service.
Six-digit date the SNM's active service is to expire.

-- Block 13 - HOME OF RECORD: Legal home of record as
listed in MCTFS.

-- Block 14 - PGM CODE: Program Code. Male applicants
use 5A followed by either (A) for aviation or (G) for
ground option. Female applicants use 5AW.

-- Block 16 - PFT SCORE: Provide total points attained and
number of pull ups, number of crunches, and run time.

-- Block 17 - WAIVERS REQUIRED: Enlistment waivers must be
renewed. Use the following codes: AY - AGE; CY - TEST SCORES;
DD - Moral; DG - Drug; DH - Alcohol; and HY - Physical.

-- Block 18 - FY: Fiscal Year.

-- Block 19 - PROJ COMM: Projected commission date. Use the
dates provided in the annual MARADMIN announcing the selection
board schedule.

SERVICE AGREEMENT
MERITORIOUS COMMISSIONING PROGRAM (GROUND OFFICER)
==
1. In connection with my nomination for enrollment in the *MERITORIOUS COMMISSIONING PROGRAM (GROUND OFFICER)* of the United States Marine Corps, I hereby acknowledge:

    a. That final approval of my nomination for enrollment in the Meritorious Commissioning Program, as an officer candidate, will be determined by the Commandant of the Marine Corps.

    b. That upon reporting to an officer candidate class, I will be required to participate in training for a minimum period of seven weeks, unless sooner disenrolled for cause, before any voluntary request for disenrollment will be considered.

    c. That, as a regular Marine, if I fail to satisfactorily complete the requirements for appointment to commissioned grade or request disenrollment from an officer candidate class prior to acceptance of a commission, I will be required to complete my enlistment contract, including any extension thereof and any obligated period of extended active duty.

    d. That, as a reserve Marine, if I am released from the AR Program to attend OCS, I realize if I fail to satisfactorily complete the requirements for appointment to commissioned grade or request disenrollment from an officer candidate class prior to acceptance of a commission, I will not be returned to active duty with the AR Program. I understand my status will be that of a member of the Individual Ready Reserve.

    e. That, upon satisfactory completion of all requirements, I will accept appointment to commissioned grade in the United States Marine Corps Reserve, if a commission is tendered to me.

    f. That:

        (1) A commission in the Marine Corps Reserve is for an indefinite term and is held during the pleasure of the President;

        (2) Upon acceptance of a commission, I will be required to serve at least eight years in the Marine Corps Reserve from date of appointment to commissioned grade;

    (3) Any portion of this eight-year period not served on active duty will be served on inactive duty as a member of the Marine Corps Reserve; and

    (4) A resignation of my reserve commission submitted prior to completion of this eight-year period will normally be rejected and, after this period, may be accepted or rejected by the President as the needs of the service may then require.

    g. Upon acceptance of appointment to commissioned grade, I will be further assigned to The Basic School for commissioned officer training.

    h. Assignment to an officer candidate class should not be construed as approval for future assignment to flight or aviation training.

    i. Sections 671a and 671b of Title 10, United States Code, currently provide as follows:

    "671a. Members: service extension during war. Unless terminated at an earlier date by the Secretary concerned, the period of active service of any member of an armed force is extended for the duration of any war in which the United States may be engaged and for six months thereafter.

    "671b. Members: service extension when Congress is not in session.

    "(a) Notwithstanding any other provision of law when the President determines that the national interest so requires, he may, if Congress is not in session, having adjourned *sine die*, authorize the Secretary of Defense to extend for not more than six months enlistments, appointments, periods of active duty, periods of obligated service or other military status, in any component of the Armed Forces of the United States, that expire before the thirtieth day after Congress next convenes or reconvenes.

    "(b) An extension under this section continues until the sixtieth day after Congress next convenes or reconvenes or until expiration of the period of extension specified by the Secretary of Defense, whichever occurs earlier, unless sooner terminated by law or Executive Order."

j. Federal statutes and pertinent regulations applicable to personnel in the Marine Corps may change without notice and that such changes may affect my status as an officer candidate or commissioned officer and obligations to serve as such.

2. I consent to serve on extended active duty, as a commissioned officer, for a minimum of three and one-half years from the date of appointment to commissioned grade, and understand that a request for release from active duty prior to completion of this period will be rejected.

3. I have read and completely understand the meaning and content of the above. Furthermore, I have read and understand the current Marine Corps Order pertaining to this program. No promises, either written or oral, have been made to me in connection with my nomination for enrollment in the Meritorious Commissioning Program (Ground Officer) except as specified above. I acknowledge receipt of a copy of this document.

Signature of Witnessing Officer   Signature of Nominee

_____   _____
Typed Name, Grade, SSN of Witness   Typed Name, SSN of Nominee

_____
Date

APPENDIX C to
ENCLOSURE (2)

3

SERVICE AGREEMENT
MERITORIOUS COMMISSIONING PROGRAM (NAVAL AVIATOR)
==

1. In connection with my nomination for enrollment in the *MERITORIOUS COMMISSIONING PROGRAM (NAVAL AVIATOR)* of the United States Marine Corps, I hereby acknowledge:

    a. That final approval of my nomination for enrollment in the Meritorious Commissioning Program (Naval Aviator), as an officer candidate, will be determined by the Commandant of the Marine Corps.

    b. That upon reporting to an officer candidate class, I will be required to participate in training for a minimum period of seven weeks, unless sooner disenrolled for cause, before any voluntary request for disenrollment will be considered.

    c. That, as a regular Marine, if I fail to satisfactorily complete the requirements for appointment to commissioned grade or request disenrollment from an officer candidate class prior to acceptance of a commission, I will be required to complete my enlistment contract, including any extension thereof and any obligated period of extended active duty.

    d. That, as a reserve Marine, if I am released from the AR Program to attend OCS, I realize if I fail to satisfactorily complete the requirements for appointment to commissioned grade or request disenrollment from an officer candidate class prior to acceptance of a commission, I will not be returned to active duty with the AR Program. I understand my status will be that of a member of the Individual Ready Reserve.

    e. That, upon satisfactory completion of all requirements, I will accept appointment to commissioned grade in the United States Marine Corps Reserve, if a commission is tendered to me.

    f. That:

        (1) A commission in the Marine Corps Reserve is for an indefinite term and is held during the pleasure of the President;

        (2) Upon acceptance of a commission, I will be required to serve at least eight years in the Marine Corps Reserve from date of appointment to commissioned grade;

(3) Any portion of this eight-year period not served on active duty will be served on inactive duty as a member of the Marine Corps Reserve; and

(4) A resignation of my reserve commission submitted prior to completion of this eight-year period will normally be rejected and, after this period, may be accepted or rejected by the President as the needs of the service may then require.

g. Upon successful completion of the officer candidate course and acceptance of appointment to commissioned grade, I will be further assigned MOS 7599 (Naval Aviator Student) and will be assigned to The Basic School for commissioned officer training prior to my assignment to flight training.

h. Upon successful completion of The Basic School, I will be assigned to Student Naval Aviator Training, provided I am physically qualified for such assignment at that time.

i. Sections 671a and 671b of Title 10, United States Code, currently provide as follows:

"671a. Members: service extension during war. Unless terminated at an earlier date by the Secretary concerned, the period of active service of any member of an armed force is extended for the duration of any war in which the United States may be engaged and for six months thereafter.

"671b. Members: service extension when Congress is not in session.

"(a) Notwithstanding any other provision of law when the President determines that the national interest so requires, he may, if Congress is not in session, having adjourned *sine die*, authorize the Secretary of Defense to extend for not more than six months enlistments, appointments, periods of active duty, periods of obligated service or other military status, in any component of the Armed Forces of the United States, that expire before the thirtieth day after Congress next convenes or reconvenes.

"(b) An extension under this section continues until the sixtieth day after Congress next convenes or reconvenes or until expiration of the period of extension specified by the Secretary of Defense, whichever occurs earlier, unless sooner terminated by law or Executive Order."

    j. Federal statutes and pertinent regulations applicable to personnel in the Marine Corps may change without notice and that such changes may affect my status as an officer candidate or commissioned officer and obligations to serve as such.

2. I consent to serve on extended active duty, as a commissioned officer, for the following minimum periods and understand that a request for release from active duty prior to completion of these minimum periods will normally be rejected:

    a. Ninety-six months from date of designation as a Naval Aviator if trained as a fixed wing pilot.

    b. Seventy-two months from date of designation as a Naval Aviator if trained as a rotary wing pilot.

3. I have read and completely understand the meaning and content of the above. Furthermore, I have read and understand the current Marine Corps Order pertaining to this program. No promises, either written or oral, have been made to me in connection with my nomination for enrollment in the Meritorious Commissioning Program (Naval Aviator) except as specified above. I acknowledge receipt of a copy of this document.

Signature of Witnessing Officer   Signature of Nominee

_____   _____

Typed Name, Grade, SSN of Witness   Typed Name, SSN of Nominee

_____

   Date

DATA SHEET

INSTRUCTIONS: This enclosure is to be locally reproduced.
Complete items A through M in column 2. Type in ALL CAPS, no
punctuation.

COLUMN 1   COLUMN 2

A. FULL NAME: (LAST FIRST MI)

B. SSN: (no spaces)

C. PRESENT GRADE:

D. PRESENT MOS:

E. RACE/ETHNIC CODE: (see BIR)

F. AGE:
    (As of date of projected commission)

G. EL/SAT/ACT TEST SCORES

H. PFT SCORE

    NO. OF PULL-UPS

    NO. OF CRUNCHES

    RUN TIME

I. LAST COLLEGE ATTENDED

J. MAJOR SUBJECT

K. CUMULATIVE GRADE POINT AVERAGE

L. EXPECTED GRADUATION DATE

M. TIME IN SERVICE:
    (As of date of nomination)

SAMPLE REPORT OF LOCAL INTERVIEW BOARD

(To be completed by the local interview board on each nominee
for the Meritorious Commissioning Program.)

1. Command convening board: (List full address)

    _____

    _____

2. Name of nominee: _____

                        (Last) (First) (M.I.)

                        _____

                        (Grade/Rank) (SSN) (MOS)

3. Date of present grade: _____

4. The nominee named above appeared before the interview board
on (date) and the following comments constitute the opinion of a
majority of the members.

    a. MANNER, APPEARANCE, BEARING: (Comment appropriately on
the nominee's military presence, appearance, and bearing. Is it
above, below, or at the standard generally expected of a Marine
officer?)

    b. VOICE, LANGUAGE EXPRESSION, ALERTNESS, ABILITY TO
COMMUNICATE: (Comment appropriately on the nominee's ability
to convey clear, concise, and intelligent expressions. Does the
nominee readily understand the meaning of questions?)

    c. PROFESSIONAL KNOWLEDGE: (Comment on the nominee's
military proficiency, general knowledge of the Marine Corps,
social and civic awareness.)

    d. SELF-CONFIDENCE, PERSONALITY, MOTIVATION: (Comment on
the nominee's degree of self-confidence, exhibited personality,
and motivation for commission.)

    e. OTHER QUALIFICATIONS: (Does the nominee possess qualifications,
not previously reported, that would be of particular value as an officer?)

APPENDIX E to
ENCLOSURE (2)

1

5. <u>RECOMMENDATION</u>: (Name of Nominee) is recommended with (enthusiasm) (confidence) (reservation) or (not recommended) for appointment to commissioned grade as a second lieutenant in the U.S. Marine Corps Reserve. (Make a summary evaluation of the nominee's qualifications and potential for commissioned service.)

6. <u>MEMBERS OF THE INTERVIEW BOARD</u>:

Member: (Full name, grade, component)

Member: (Full name, grade, component)

Member: (Full name, grade, component)

_____
Signature of Senior Member

APPENDIX E to
ENCLOSURE (2)

ACADEMIC CERTIFICATION FOR THE MERITORIOUS COMMISSIONING PROGRAM
===
NAME OF STUDENT | SOCIAL SECURITY NUMBER
_____|_____

COLLEGE OR UNIVERSITY

_____

     This is to certify that the above named subject:

     Was _____ / Was not _____ a regularly enrolled full-time
student at this institution.

     The above named Student has _____ / has not _____ completed
the requirement for an Associate Degree.

     Date of completion of degree requirements _____

     The below information is required to determine this student's
eligibility for admission to, or retention in, the U.S Marine
Corps Meritorious Commissioning Program:

     MAJOR SUBJECT _____
     TOTAL NUMBER OF HOURS ATTEMPTED _____
     TOTAL NUMBER OF HOURS COMPLETED _____
     TOTAL NUMBER OF GRADE POINTS ACHIEVED _____
     CUMULATIVE GRADE POINT AVERAGE (GPA) _____

     AT THIS INSTITUTION A GPA OF _____
     IS EQUIVALENT TO A "C".

     SAT SCORE: MATH _____ VERBAL _____
     ACT SCORE: MATH _____ ENGLISH _____

   It is requested that a certified copy of the student's
transcript be returned with this form.

     REMARKS:

             SIGNATURE _____
     PLEASE
     AFFIX   TITLE _____
     SEAL
                  DATE _____

MCO 1040.43A
2 May 00

COMPLETE MAILING ADDRESS
OF COLLEGE/UNIVERSITY
INCLUDING ZIP CODE

Dear Registrar,

The student whose name appears on the enclosed form has been
nominated for enrollment in the U.S. Marine Corps Meritorious
Commissioning Program. Since a minimum grade point average is
required for admission to, or retention in our programs, I am
requesting your cooperation in furnishing essential information
on this individual's academic status.

I realize many demands are made upon your time, but please be
assured the Marine Corps relies on this information in the
decision process.

Enclosed is an addressed, postage-free envelope for your
convenience in returning this form.

                                    Sincerely,

===
I am aware of the provisions of the Family Education Rights
Act. I hereby authorize the release of the requested information
and an official transcript directly to the Marine Corps agency
indicated on this form.

_____   _____   _____
(Signature of Witness)   (Signature of Nominee)   (Date)

APPENDIX F to
ENCLOSURE (2)

COMMON PROBLEMS WITH MEDICAL FORMS

1. <u>Standard Form 88, Report of Medical Examination</u>

   a. Marks and Scars must be listed. Tattoos, brandings, body piercings, etc, must be identified and appropriate color photographs submitted. Do not send photos of private areas.

   b. Dental block must be completed. Do not send x-rays.

   c. EKG is required. A baseline EKG is acceptable. Provide a copy of the EKG Printout which includes interpretation by the doctor.

   d. Must contain the HIV AIDS Test results and date tested. HIV drawn or pending is not acceptable. If not drawn at time of physical examination, include a copy of the Chronological Record of HIV Testing or LAB printout from VIROMED LABS.

   e. Blood Pressure (sitting position) readings must not be higher than 140/90. If either systolic or diastolic reading is outside the limit, submit 3-day blood pressure readings. If hypertension is indicated, provide a current Internal Medicine Evaluation.

   f. Distant vision must be corrected to 20/20. If eyesight is other than 20/20, must include a manifest refraction. The statement "by lenses" is not acceptable.

   g. Audiogram must be completed. If any readings are outside the normal range, submit a repeat audiogram and an ear, nose, and throat (ENT) consultation.

2. <u>Standard Form 93, Report of Medical History</u>

   a. Affirmative answers to questions on SF93 must be explained by the physician in the notes section and supporting documents submitted. Only qualified applicants will be considered by the board.

   b. All medical forms must be dated and signed by both the applicant and the physician.

3. Aviation applicants must have, in addition to the above, a contact lens statement, anthropometric measurements, cycloplegic refraction, and other flight tests per reference (c).

INFORMATION FOR COMMANDING OFFICERS

1. <u>Background</u>. The enlisted-to-officer commissioning programs supplement civilian source officer procurement efforts by providing the Marine Corps with an excellent base of unrestricted officers. ECP and MCP candidates report to OCS with varying degrees of mental and physical readiness. This readiness, or lack of it, is a direct reflection of a strong or weak command precommission- ing training. Such command interest is an important factor in the attitude with which the candidate enters training. Many voluntary requests for disenrollment can be avoided if the new candidate has been given personal supervision by a knowledgeable officer.

2. The list below provides helpful suggestions by which commanding officers may monitor and motivate approved candidates within the command prior to reporting to OCS.

   a. Have candidates briefed on precommissioning training by a locally assigned lieutenant, if available, who is a recent graduate of The Basic School. Women applicants should be briefed by a woman officer, whenever possible. Additionally, there are officer selection officers (OSOs) stationed at MCB Camp Lejeune and MCB Camp Pendleton who can be called upon for information. These OSOs can provide the candidate with an insight into the selection process and mentor him or her prior to reporting to OCS. OSS LANT can be reached at DSN: 751-0126, OSS WRR can be reached at DSN: 361-0268.

   b. Have candidates participate in a daily monitored program which has both variety and concentration on physical fitness. Emphasis should be placed on endurance exercises such as running, upper body development (both of which should be on occasion completed in boots), and circuit training.

   c. Encourage candidates to read the OCS Handout and OCS Preparation Guide which are mailed to all selectees for the program.

ENCLOSURE (4)